Sponges Are Skeletons

BY **Barbara Juster Esbensen** · ILLUSTRATED BY **Holly Keller**

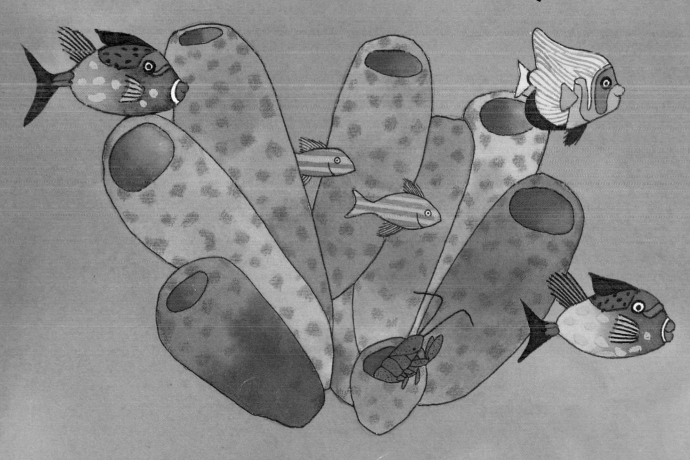

HarperCollins*Publishers*

The *Let's-Read-and-Find-Out Science Book* series was originated by Dr. Franklyn M. Branley, Astronomer Emeritus and former Chairman of the American Museum–Hayden Planetarium, and was formerly co-edited by him and Dr. Roma Gans, Professor Emeritus of Childhood Education, Teachers College, Columbia University. For a complete catalog of Let's-Read-and-Find-Out Science Books, write to HarperCollins Children's Books, 10 East 53rd Street, New York, NY 10022.

Let's Read-and-Find-Out Science Book is a registered trademark of HarperCollins Publishers.

Library of Congress Cataloging-in-Publication Data
Esbensen, Barbara Juster.
   Sponges are skeletons / by Barbara Juster Esbensen ; illustrated by
Holly Keller.
      p.   cm. — (Let's-read-and-find-out science book)
   Summary: Explains how sponges are animals that live in the ocean
and how they are harvested and used by humans.
   ISBN 0-06-021034-6. — ISBN 0-06-021037-0 (lib. bdg.)
   1. Sponges—Juvenile literature. [1. Sponges.] I. Keller, Holly, ill.
II. Title. III. Series.
QL371.6.E73 1993   92-9740
593.4—dc20   CIP
                                                        AC

Sponges Are Skeletons

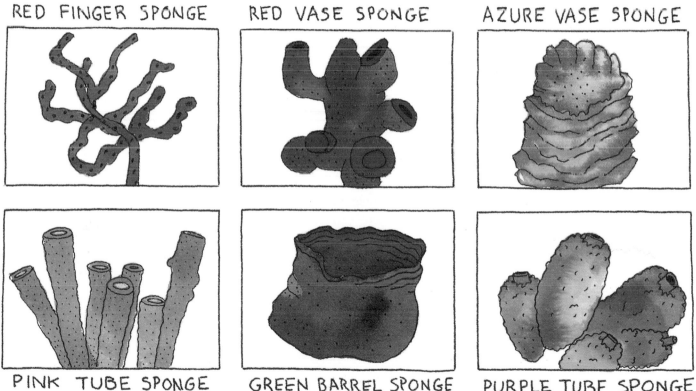

RED FINGER SPONGE   RED VASE SPONGE   AZURE VASE SPONGE

PINK TUBE SPONGE   GREEN BARREL SPONGE   PURPLE TUBE SPONGE

Bath time!

Time for water and soap.

And a sponge.

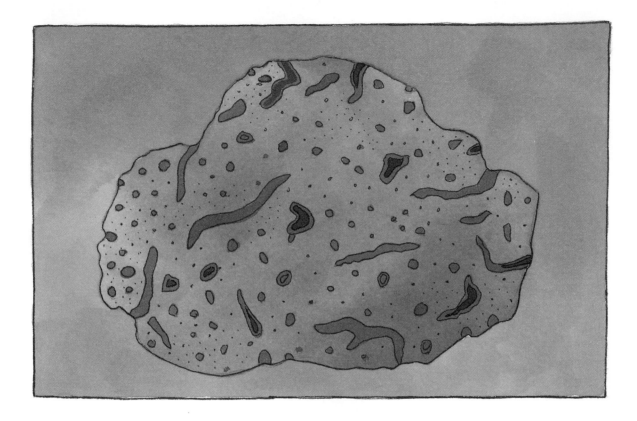

A sponge is especially good for washing because it holds more water than a washcloth. A sponge is full of holes and tunnels. The water goes into all the holes and tunnels until you squeeze it out.

Pick up the sponge. Now plunge it under the water. Watch it fill up. The sponge is heavy now. Squeeze it. *Sploosh! Splash! Dribble!* The bathwater rains down on you.

When you squeeze a sponge, you are squeezing the soft skeleton of an animal. This animal once lived in the salty waters of the sea.

You have a skeleton inside your body. It is made of hard bones, and it gives your body its shape. The skeleton that is a bath sponge is made of a soft material called spongin. This soft skeleton gives the sponge its bumpy shape.

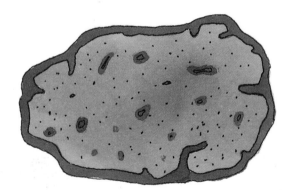

A sponge is an animal that lives in the sea. But sponges are different from many other animals in two important ways.

First, a sponge cannot move from place to place to get its food. Sponges grow attached to rocks, other animals, even shipwrecks.

Second, sponges do not have special body parts like most animals do. A sponge does not have a heart. It does not have a mouth or a stomach. Sponges do not have lungs to help them breathe. The water they live in brings them everything they need. It brings them food. It brings them the oxygen they need to stay alive.

When it was alive, the sponge was almost round. Its soft skeleton was covered with a skin that looked like leather. The skin was filled with holes. The holes are called pores.

Pores are very important to a living sponge. When the sponge was alive, it pumped sea water through its thousands of small pores. Tiny plants in the water were food for the sponge. The food in the water moved inside the tunnels and chambers in the sponge's body.

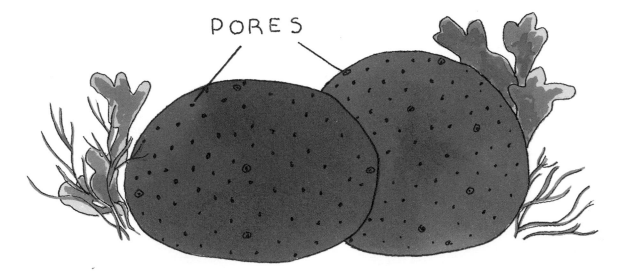

PORES

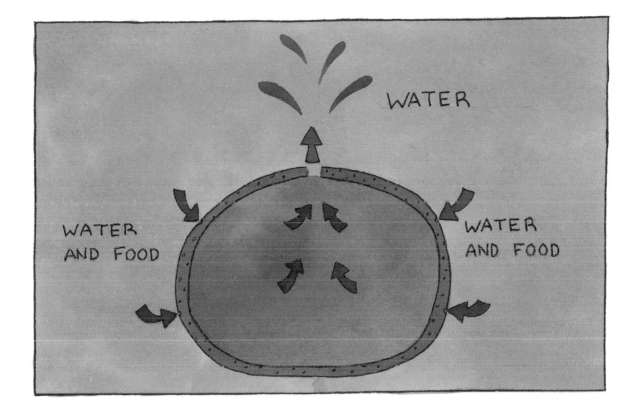

Then the water was pumped out through one or more large holes. The food was left behind. The sponge acts as a filter. It feeds on the tiny plants and other things that are in the water. The sponge helps to keep the water of the ocean clear and clean.

Sponges do not look like animals. For many years, people thought they were sea plants. Divers do an experiment to show that the sponge is an animal that can pump water through its body. They put colored dye in the water at the bottom of a tube sponge. In only a few seconds, the colored water shoots out of the top. The sponge has pumped the water through its body.

The holes in the sponge protect many sea animals that live in them. Pistol shrimp, small fish, brittle stars, tiny crabs, and lobsters all find safety inside a sponge. Sponges are homes to all these sea animals.

Scientists think that sponges have been living under the seas for 700 million years. If you could dive into every ocean in the world, you would be able to find some kind of sponge growing there.

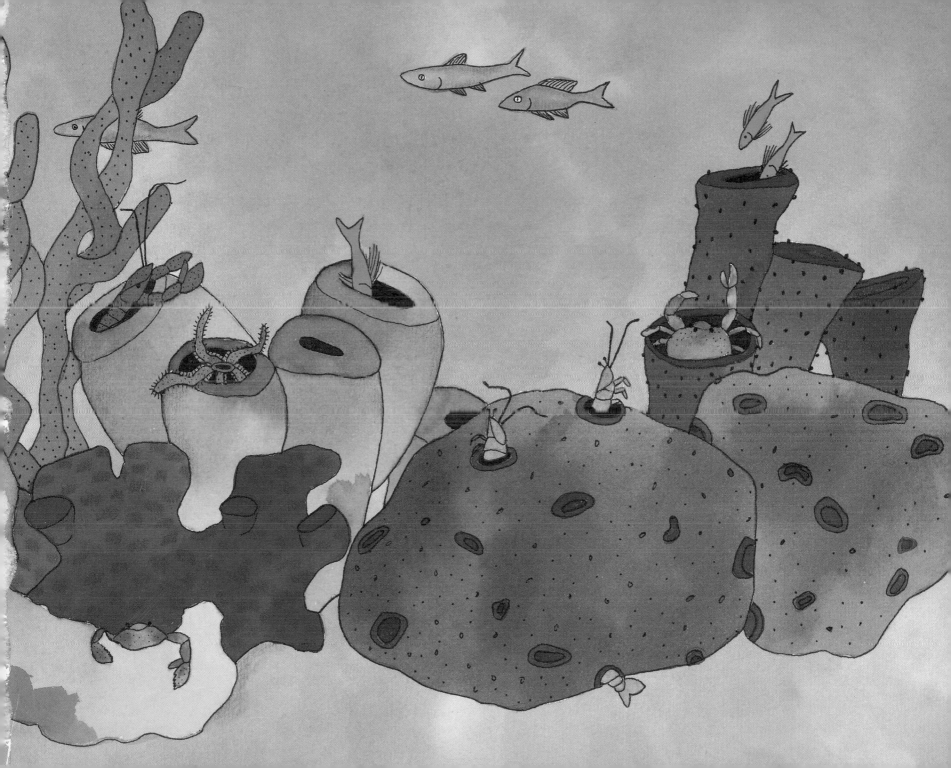

ELEPHANT EAR
SPONGE

MOOSE ANTLER
SPONGE

Sponges have been given different names. Sometimes the name describes the way a sponge looks: elephant's ear sponge, moose antler sponge.

Often the name tells us how the sponge feels on your skin when it is wet: wool sponge, velvet sponge. The softest sponge is called silk sponge. Can you imagine how this wet sponge would feel on your face?

Some sponge skeletons are made of small glassy needles instead of soft spongin. They would not be good to wash with!

Your bath sponge has many relatives under the sea. Under water, sponges all seem to be the same soft blue color. But using lights, divers have seen blazing red sponges. They have seen bright yellow ones. Some sponges are glowing purple. Others are brilliant blue.

Most sponges lose their color when they are brought to the surface and die. We can see their living beauty only in pictures the divers bring back for us.

Sponges come in different sizes and shapes. There is a sponge no bigger than a bean. One sponge grows to be so large that a diver can climb inside it and peek over the edge. Instead of having a sponge in your bath, you could have a bath in your sponge!

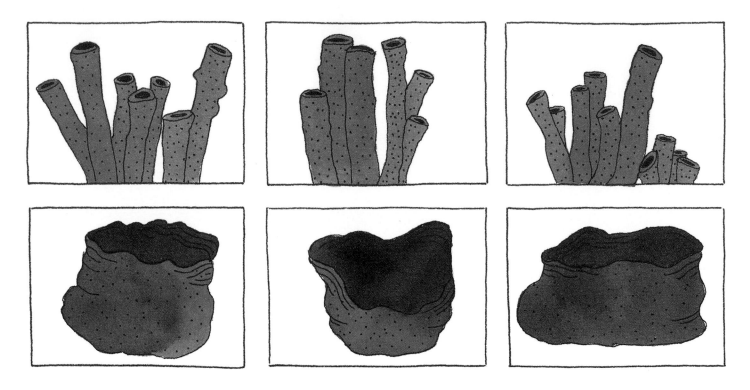

No two living sponges are ever exactly the same shape. Every living sponge looks a bit different from every other one. Some sponges live to be hundreds of years old.

Most things we call sponges today were never alive. They do not come from the sea. They come from a factory.

In a factory, sponges can be made out of rubber and other

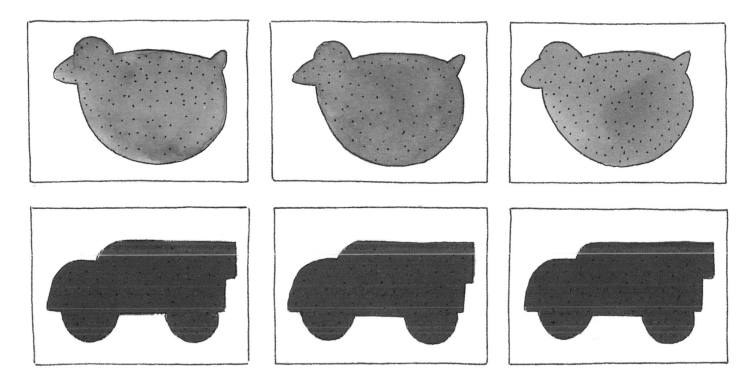

materials. The factory can cut the material into thousands of
duck shapes. Or firetruck shapes. All of the duck-shaped sponges
will be exactly alike. All of the firetruck sponges will be exactly
alike.

Many people would rather use a natural sponge than a rubber
one, especially for bathing.

Sponge fishermen bring up our bath sponges from deep in the ocean water.

Greek sponge fishermen came to Tarpon Springs in Florida almost one hundred years ago. They found sponges with soft skeletons on the ocean floor off of Florida's west coast. All of the sponges harvested in the United States are taken from these sponge beds. Most of the divers are members of those first Greek families.

Sometimes, divers must go as deep as one hundred feet to harvest the sponges. The sponges are harvested with hooks. They are loosened from the bottom of the ocean and put into big nets. Then they are brought up to the deck of the boat.

The sponges are piled on the deck and covered with wet cloths. The sponges die and their skins rot. The smell is terrible—*whew*!

The fishermen wash the sponge skeletons clean. Then they string them up to dry. They look like huge necklaces drying in the sun. Later they are cleaned again. Now the sponges are ready to be used by painters or car washers or for any cleaning job.

But your bath sponge is cleaned many more times, to make it much softer for you to enjoy.

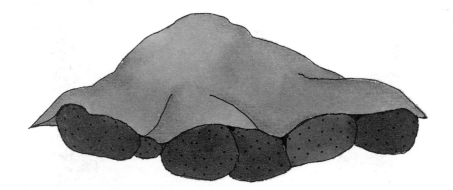

Sploosh! Splash! Dribble! Time to squeeze a skeleton. Have a good bath!